RES PUBLICA

PHOENIX **POETS**

A SERIES EDITED BY ALAN SHAPIRO

ALAN WILLIAMSON

res publica

THE UNIVERSITY OF CHICAGO PRESS
Chicago and London

Alan Williamson is professor of English at the University of California, Davis. He is the author of three previous books of poems, most recently *Love and the Soul,* and three books of criticism. His poetry has appeared in the *Paris Review*, the *American Poetry Review*, *Ploughshares*, *Poetry*, and the *Yale Review*.

The University of Chicago Press, Chicago 60637
The University of Chicago Press, Ltd., London
© 1998 by The University of Chicago
All rights reserved. Published 1998
Printed in the United States of America

07 06 05 04 03 02 01 00 99 98   1 2 3 4 5

ISBN 0-226-89934-9 (cloth)
         0-226-89935-7 (paper)

Library of Congress Cataloging-in-Publication Data

Williamson, Alan (Alan Bacher), 1944–
         Res publica / Alan Williamson.
              p.   cm. — (Phoenix poets)
         Includes bibliographical references (p. 73).
         ISBN 0-226-89934-9 (alk. paper). — ISBN 0-226-89935-7 (pbk. :
    alk. paper)
         I. Title.   II. Series.
         PS3573.I45623R4   1998
         811'.54 — dc21   98 - 11462
                                                                          CIP

Contents

Acknowledgments

Poems from this collection have appeared in the following periodicals and anthologies:

AGNI: "Altamont," "Listening to Leonard Cohen"
Barnabe Mountain Review: "After 'Death of a Porn Queen': Traveling the Great Basin"
Blind Donkey: Journal of the Diamond Sangha: "Ikkyu" (vol. 14, no. 2)
Canto: "Montale: Times at Bellosguardo"
Marlboro Review: "Linda Does My Horoscope"
Michigan Quarterly Review: "La Pastorela" (vol. 36, no. 1)
Northeast Corridor (based at Beaver College, Glenside, PA): "After the Election, 1984"
Poetry: "Puccini Dying"
Slate Magazine: "The Lighthouse"
Southwest Review: "The Wall of June"
Tikkun Magazine, A Bi-Monthly Jewish Critique of Politics, Culture, and Society (San Francisco, CA): "A Childhood Around 1950," reprinted with permission
TriQuarterly: "Red Cloud"
Virginia Quarterly Review: "Dinosaurs," *"In Paradiso, speriamo bene"*
Yale Review: "Dreams of Sacrifice"

I am grateful to Leonard Cohen for permission to quote from "Suzanne" and "Bird on a Wire"; and to Sonja Arntzen for permission to borrow a few lines, as well as much information, from her *Ikkyu and the Crazy Cloud Anthology: A Zen Poet of Medieval Japan.* Again, I must thank the John Simon Guggenheim Memorial Foundation; and friends, far too many to name.

I
RES PUBLICA

A Childhood Around 1950

Sometimes a horse pulled a wagon down the street.
A knife-grinder sometimes knocked at the back door.
Airplanes passed over. Put to bed in the poignant
half-thereness of summer twilights, we followed their long wobble
into Midway, rare and slow as dragonflies.

New kinds of safety. Our parents held their breath,
though sickness, for us, was the vile yellow powders
that burst from the capsules we had to gulp, and couldn't.
The new danger quiet in the milk and air.

The electric chair troubled no one. Good and evil
were stark things, as grainy movies made the dark.
But the city stopped if one of us was stolen,
and found thrown, days later, in a forest preserve.

It was what was. A childhood always is.
Fathers came home at noon and took off their hats.
Later, streetlights . . . But who was that *lamplighter,* in the stories?
And we went on living it, like a wave, that doesn't know
it is at every moment different water.

The Cusp

Nasals praising Geritol
in *Quiz Show,* not
yet exposed: so vulgar
they seem innocent, like
the high round-fendered cars
nosing west again
on the unrationed gas
after the War was over . . .

Sputnik made our country
love learning; though as the villain
leans forward and confides to us,
"Really it's the *money*!"

Then Castro—Todd Gitlin
so right about this—haranguing
on the same bluish screens
the first wedge driven: why didn't
the Senators trust his beard?
Why wasn't he the "freedom"

we'd learned to huddle under
our schooldesks to defend
when the air-raid siren blew
each Tuesday at ten-thirty?
Or the time my friend and I
imagined and then believed
a low-flying plane
was the Russians coming . . .

                    Nowhere

to break to: the squat
blackened Norman towers
of Stagg Field where the first
chain-reaction happened
so beautiful, that moment,
against the old sky.

Dreams of Sacrifice

(Chicago, April 1968)

I saw them coming, waves of them—from the West Side
we'd watched burning on TV—up the dim treads
in the tarnished-gold light I'd loved, if I were honest,
every year of my life; then down the landing,
yelling, brandishing, surging, toward our door . . .
And saw myself come out, chest bare—
not really, but as if my heart walked bare before me,
saying, "Take me for all of us, wash me, make me yours,
make me pure enough to do your will for all;
or if not, kill me."

         Three weeks later, they (well, one of them)
did kill someone like me, and my parents heard it,
the lone shot the bicyclist fired, that sent the body
crumpling against the railing of my old school.
They were "sick" that they "mistook the shot for a backfire."
And, perhaps because I'd been so absolute,
that spring break, about fascist "Amerika,"
they sent me the clipping, the faces. Though he'd had little
enough sympathy for me, when he used to watch
white toughs dog me home along that same
spear-pointed fence, my father wrote, "the victim,
a benevolent student . . ."

I suppose the face reminded me
too much of my own, pudgy, irresolute, *in search of,*
ashamed of, innocence—so I wrote, needing
to *make claims* for the hungry bones of that other face,
tilted up to police lights, floating, high,
whose *single beauty* lay in killing *one*
for one, one for the shared, blurred guilt of all.

My father, too, it seemed, needed some way
to place himself. Already ill,
he walked out the half block, one quick May night,
"to see the spot where trees cast a dense shadow."
I imagined *blackness lay focussed,* for him,
like a body crumpled there; and wrote my poem
to prove his dark was created by light,
light looking *too tenderly* at itself—the windows
of our building bent back that way, by the crenellations—
light streaming on his back, what he wouldn't see, the *clue* . . .

When you're young, your world's imposed on you, so powerful
against you, you think it's all-powerful, forever—
easy enough to side with its destroyers.
But when it's half-vanished, and freighted with
everything you've loved and achieved within it,
easy to make of love and achievement a fist, to smash
whatever hurts your world . . .

                    Avalokiteshvara
split his head in ten, with meditating
on the ways of suffering. In the old bronze,
you can see the heads dangling, like bluebells on a stalk,
the eleventh flowering on top
because, the way they tell the story, the Buddha
could still put them back together, and add his own.

Paint It Black

It was clearer then
how there's a depth in longing
nothing ever reaches. Geoffrey and I sat up talking

in the bare apartment, the streets
sunk beyond leaf-depth
in their two, three hours of absolute

quiet. I was angry
because I'd botched something—the very
drunk, beautiful teenaged townie

bound for Goucher in the fall
who drove us harrowingly up over
brick sidewalks, whose focus

on me I didn't pick up on till too late.
Geoffrey thinks, in such cases,
you don't get a second chance. Perhaps

I'm more restless than really angry,
the way, in the oddly triumphant drive
of *Paint It Black,* that summer,

you never know what—
infidelity, death?—has made him
want to see, where her face was, the Black Sun.

(Later, I'd see her
laughing too much, in the coffeehouses,
with a skeletal African dancer

suspected, next year,
of rifling purses and lifting my twenty-first birthday watch
at another "open party.") But for now

it's very late. The dew
gathers on the strange backyard power-stations,
on every rotting plank of the three-deckers.

Suddenly a long shaking
comes through the ground, followed
(measurably) by a clap like thunder. Next day

we'll learn it was liquid hydrogen
in the Electron Accelerator at Harvard
two blocks away. Four technicians

critically burned—like sacrifices
in the underground caves
of Teotihuacan where the snake-faces

conch shells and wave-signs climb the stairs to the sun.
What I can't forget
is how, when it happened, when we ran

outside to nothing at all—dawn beginning—
I knew I'd been
waiting for it, some coded

burst from the core. These small hours
I think of the years (X's breasts
that made me feel no straining, but like a tree

outfeathering; *Y* imaginarily
glimpsed in the museum) and still
reach down for it, hand under

the roots . . .

Listening to Leonard Cohen

(driving south from Charlottesville, January 1993)

In the dawn of time I lived on a little hill.
It was green even in January, green up to
the doorstep where, short weeks later, a miniature
hyacinth would come. The lines of the house were neat
as a jewelbox, from which, in the pearly, brooding days,
freshness had spilled. And, of course, we who lived there
found ways to be unhappy.
                                        All men would
be sailors in those years. They wanted the landscape
to fold to a wave-length; wanted not to know
when they woke in the morning, which state's light was broken
through the slant pines. Wanted the afternoons
in shade-pulled rooms to bring girls whose eyes
were that wide with possibility, shocked free; whose very names
they wouldn't learn. (And the women wanting?—not that,
but not to be kept in houses.)
                                        And we, who'd begun
to hold still, like our parents, half from fear,
half from hope of taking root—
after Altamont, after Manson, we were afraid
of our own side, no less than of their opposites
who looked just like them, mountain men, the dirty
runnels of time their beards.

There is a grain of sand in Lambeth that Satan cannot find
Nor can his Watch Fiends find it tho' they search numbering every grain
(But who were the Watch Fiends? And was it here, on the hill,
or only there where everything changes?) *for within*
Opening into Beulah every angle a lovely heaven . . .
Playing perhaps as I sat reading this, *heroes in*
the seaweed, children in the morning—

                                        making me wish for a guide
to the spaces inside the moment, someone I loved
without having to love her, because she
was water wave-length madness *oranges from China,*
the river's endless answer out her door . . .

And so, to the open-air rock bands; at the medievalist's
old stage-inn lost in the country—angry at the roles
we were trying to become, angry at our selves
too small to be or reject them (so the large
ghosts waited, armed, at the limits where our sight
failed, out the night door)—we kept asking the songs
to tell us about change. When were they too long, dwindling
down hillslope distance?

                              When R. D. Laing
lectured on Jefferson's Lawn, the newer young ones drew us,
in their protest leaflet, with tangled snakes for hair
and Picasso slippage, double nose and eyes . . .
And what they wanted as the woodblock Jesus,
square beard and brow, square and blunt even the line
between Him and His Star; to whom "the Rapture"
meant the day that we, the Lost, would seek them
room to room and street to street, learning too late
the God they served had snatched them bodily out
of all this, before letting loose the fire . . .

Then Janis: "Oh Lord won't you buy me
a Mercedes Benz"—her scrawny voice an angel's
unaccompanied trumpet—

                        & the world slept in Ulro.

Twenty years, Leonard Cohen . . . New sounds in the street: the dog
strangled in mid-yelp that means that someone's
turned off a car alarm. Soft ringing
of an early-shopping cart, picking up bottles
before the recycling van.

                    New viruses, early cancers
the price perhaps for the antibiotic nimbus
of childhoods where no friends died, that let us carry
our young looks so fresh and far into middle age . . .

I saw a beggar leaning on his wooden crutch,
He said to me, You must not ask for so much,
And a pretty woman leaning in her darkened door,
She cried to me, Hey why not ask for more?

Shapeshifter voice, yearning and shrugging off—
insight that should hold and kill, gone down the flood—
I would step twice in the eternal river, if I could,
with you, with Suzanne, with William Blake of Lambeth,
where every atom lives, the most fleeting love is answered,
every moment is fire, each singe an opening eye;
and still think it's my fault, if, at the great concert-fairs,
I never quite linked up, but always ended watching
on the ragged pathways out of afternoon
the dust give back its odd, quizzical stare.

Altamont

A stretch of highway, now, with wind-machines
for a thousand Don Quixotes
scooping against the hot emptiness of the Valley;
poisons from the weapons lab migrating underground . . .
But then, they say, the pavement was parked solid.

Then it must have looked like some Last Judgment, stunned
between bare hills and sky, the coffin-lids
upfaced beside them . . . One spectator had a vision
all present were already dead. (The paisleys
starting to look like cardboard cut-outs; faces
you still see on Telegraph, at once down-home,
childlike, and seen-it-all-in-a-hundred-lives . . .)

This is one of the places where it ended,
our dream that Hobbes was wrong, a million wills
freed of the "real" would make a counterpoint
so vast, so many-corridored, no one ever
could feel afraid there . . .
                                      Did even Deconstruction
start here, Mick Jagger "just an entertainer"
in the cold evening wind,
not Blake's voice singing from a place aflow
beyond even the wild grasses?

                        I know
two people who were there. Richard remembers
the first tendrils of the fog, driving home
with the sad talk-shows.
                              Peter describes
stepping over a hill crest just out
of sight: hundreds of men
peeing, a dozen rabbits
trying to run away.

After the Election, 1984

That glop on the window—you could call it heavy rain—
on the night ride in *Silkwood,* when Meryl Streep is telling
how her marriage just happened, abandoning her children
also just happened—and then she begins to sing
Amazing Grace that saved a wretch like me
and the camera moves outside, her face barely there through the rippling . . .
It makes me think of how we don't have last names
in public anymore; how we do so much of our shopping
to music; or the statisticians deciding
how far Reagan must praise peace, and Mondale war.
They interrupted the returns for the "Hallowe'en murderer," trim
and moustached like his captors. The wind was high,
or they were tugging him along so rapidly, through the wide
concrete spaces, but I think he said "I regret it," rather tonelessly,
not an admission, like the announcers regretting
how their East Coast projections affect the West Coast polls.
When Silkwood goes to die, she sings it again, in sunlight,
that becomes the light in the rearview mirror, pursuing,
haloing her hair; and the voice-over continues,
'Twas grace that taught my heart to fear . . .
It's the last we see of her, but something seems changed,
tenser, clearer in the air, though we know that nothing
will ever be proved; the company will buy off
the relatives with a settlement; a scriptwriter will remember
something heard in college about martyrs
or the Aztecs: their blood goes back, to refresh the sun.

Speakers from the Ice

When your hand touches a cold enough piece of metal,
it's your hand that gets torn.

                       —The ice that becomes your flesh
is gray, wide, smoky; lost in it
as on the smoky shoulders of a highway
that crosses into too many other highways,
or when the TV crosses into electric snow
and you've slid too far inside it, on the bland
announcervoices, to come back anyplace
shining with solidness—you might find yourself saying,
"When he took you, why didn't they stop the highways?"

And a voice might answer, in that cloudy   (abducted
slipping-space: "One moment it was my skateboard   child,
that wasn't, where it made sense; the next it was me.   1988)
The moments after—well, I suppose they've lived them
in their own way, drifting into my room, asking my toys
whether I lived or died. But they couldn't block the freeways,
the way you said—there are too many of us,
it would stop the traffic, even, to your door.
But it seeps back on all of you . . . My hours of happiness
aren't real now, even to me. My name is Horror."

"They'll never find you," you say. At that, the ice gets redder,
as with the blood of those who've torn their hands
free, in order to live; or as if a sightless city
ground its rusts around you. From that, another voice:

"Odd, isn't it—in our age it's the victims
who wander lost forever. Where will you find the damned?"

"Some acts have always drawn everyone to Hell,
even alive." Then, nagged by some lost headline
like a half-heard song, you add, "But don't I
          know you?"
And the silence saying you're right, you go on,   (vigilante,
"They weren't quite wrong, were they, to call you   1984)
          'gentle'?
'Machines don't hurt you,' you said, and talked to them
hours on end, soothing the least scratch of their unease
in an algebraic heaven. Was it waiting changed you,
the lonely crystal, the tetrahedron of planning?"

Then he: "You don't know. To do what everyone is thinking,
take that upon yourself. Ride in on your donkey,
idiots gawking from the trees. A whole restaurantful
paid my bill, when I came back, and felt so damned."

And you: "The city hated the smoky slippage,
which it called toleration. Of course, overcrowded prisons,
too-long dockets, even signs addressed
expressly to criminals—'This driver carries
no more than $5 in change'—are not precisely
toleration.
          But the city was on holiday
those December days, its Feast of Fools, its invisible
master bound at its feet."

"But waiting, too, for me
to trip myself, to pay for what they wanted.
The limping god, remember? *Who touches iron
is iron.* Why so many years unmarried
and fascinated with guns? Why the itchy calls to the neighbor?
Why shoot them in the back?"

"Could someone who'd rehearsed
as long as you had, ever have waited
to be really sure?"

"It was so far behind me,
so far in the past, when I actually saw it happen,
backs or fronts didn't exist. Of course I crippled
the least guilty—their obscene martyr."

"They were live flesh, too. There's more than one book about them—
the Projects, what it cost to walk down the street.
But it's you I fear for. I see you going down
the long path with its constant flashbulbs, their eerie metal
inextricably part of your veins . . .
Never to wake up and be just anyone.
Never not be part of floodlights and killing again."

And then you can hear the shrug inside his silence:
"Don't worry about me. There's much worse farther in."

And with that there's depth behind him, and a wind,
you don't know from where, but as if, beyond all warmth,
a thousand turbines blew it . . .

Images. The little   (Lockerbie,
towns of the sky fall on the towns of earth.   Scotland,
A warehouse of burnt bits two inches long,   1988–89)
where someone, slow as a child, tries to explain
how it explains it. Thin nakednesses, moving   (Treblinka,
into a snow-screen; and, again, announcervoices.   1941)
There will you find the damned? Who only speak
to telephones—

        "The heroic execution
of Flight 103 . . ."

        —or the wires, stretching   (former death camp
from the sound truck in the grim suburb (the   guard, *Shoah*)
    filmmaker
sick with numbers, sure that no promises
hold, this far down)—

        "Fur diese arme Leute   ("For these poor
war es sehr, sehr kalt"   people, it was
        The sneaked-in camera   very, very
catches the emptied features . . .   cold")
        And the wind . . .

Limit of Volume

(Kurt Cobain 1967–1994)

At the limit of volume
becoming pain
undertones appear,
we can hear them all at once—
*Antichrist in the
kitchen,* borderline
whispers of lives
that couldn't find themselves livable
without constant burnishings of the surface . . .

(Talking about "values"
when we don't mean
people plugged in to their electric toys
like life-supports;
laser arcades where the "middle class"
shoot each other—
the poor use real guns—)

Aberdeen, Washington, where it rains
all winter, where nothing
earns but the video store—
"wrong side of the
tracks," all that shit
dropping like percussion . . .

In Utero . . . the scream
at the bottom
somehow understood
all the way up.

La Pastorela

Like the first centuries. The outsiders get wind of
what's at the center, down thousands of desert miles—
the golden Empire, pulsating, tossing out
its tentacles, leaching their strength—and wanting so much
at once to share and despise it, break it down.
(Bomb-factories in New Jersey; slave-ships foundering offshore . . .)

But these are different. Their language held this place,
right for the dust-glint of olives, the waterless flame
that, from April onwards, licks across the hills
like an Inquisitor's, centuries before
they were brought here in truckloads, seasonal, the flat hot fields
another country the American highway
looks away from, like Europe from the cattle-cars.
But for ten years my mother and her friends have come
across the hills from Carmel only Arabs
and movie stars could build in now, to see them
take the old Mission for their new-old play.
And one year it even got on television:
the shepherd-girl dreaming St. Michael—Linda Ronstadt
come in shopping-mall-rainbow jewels, solar gauze,
out of the too-white California sky
to send them out on the roads to seek the Child.
The journey long as history, the eternal
gray of the ghost-sloughs, hill oaks scrubbed with winter.

The Hells Angels roaring through Hollister are remembered
in the spiked leather wristbands
the demons wear; Manson and his girls in *El Cosmico* . . .

In the campfire songs at twilight, the devil joins in,
as when does he not, on such journeys?

They've got him splendidly,
as he is, a subtle fellow; offering no
kingdoms or orgies, he gets people to see things
a little wrong, out of the steady balance
of wants and limits.

(In our multicultural
English Departments, you can hear him whisper
to the ethnic poet, the postcolonial critic,
"If they fault a line, or question a fact, it's racism;
they've been having *their* say a thousand years"—
then tell the whites, "Look how sloppy they are, how arrogant;
always getting something for nothing—that's their game.")

So he turns them all to sheep, and sends them running.

. . . In the real church, of course it's better: the Shepherd's staves
bright with crepe paper, tin cans, lanterns, feathers, flowers.
San Miguel by the altar; Lucifer at Hell-mouth
(draped over the church door); and the girl kneeling
where their rays converge . . . Lucifer (Luzbel) and Satanas
are two separate persons; Satanas is androgynous;
at Armageddon, St. Michael and Luzbel sweep in
on high-necked wooden horses, black, star-blue.
The angels bullfight the little devils, the ones whose horns
keep slipping off; then the great protagonists,
swordless, fling *brujo* magic from their palms.

At last all draws toward the altar; resonance
of whitewash on Roman arches; a real baby;
gift-giving; and the Hermit does a dance,
because he owns nothing to give. Then they file back,
an angel and a devil, two by two,
and, walking out, we shake the actors' hands.

Out into America, under the thick, full stars . . .
Does it help us accept it all? Our human lights,
thicker than stars, over what was once plain country;
a culture of quotation marks, without boundaries . . .
"When we first came," my mother says, "it was all Mexicans
and five of us; now it's the other way round."

     Accept, even, Linda Ronstadt
saying to the Devil, in her version
of biblical English, "Rise, you horrendous beast!"
—though perhaps in a thousand years some hybrid flower,
lovely with possibility as French
or Italian, will bloom out of the wreckage . . .

In the film, the shepherd girl wakes up, and finds she's
just a girl from the town; it was the scruffy old Hermit
knocked the eagle-lectern down on her head when he mounted
the pulpit; and suddenly
she was no longer watching, she was part of the play.
And she'll be different, now that she's been there
at the manger in Bethlehem, with the real Child:
in love with a young field hand, who's come in
to be one of the actors; sorry she blamed her mother
for going on having babies and keeping them poor . . .

A little north of here, someone slightly younger
didn't wake up; she was found thrown
in a scrub-wood by the highway, outside Cloverdale,
by a man let loose after serving half his sentence.
By all the bad childhoods, sealed in blue tattoos
like Satanas' wristbands? By a society
that won't believe its own moral judgments sixteen years' worth?
By the gladiatorial murders on TV?

How short a time back, we were the severe Republic,
gone back to filch learning—but also keep our distance—
from the sly old centaurs under the olive trees.
Now the sex-shops in Milan are called "Magic California."
If you were with Tacitus, and walking in
that brick market-labyrinth-arcade, near the Forum
of Trajan, where the terror
of its having happened over and over can be felt more
than in Circus or Colosseum,
what vision could you have truer than the moment
when the Devil holds up the crown of thorns on fire,
and shows (in the high-tech version) the whole future
flickering within: Calvary, the long procession
aslant the hill-ridge, like the one Death leads
in Bergman's *Seventh Seal;* the sponge, the spear;
and says, in effect, "You'll be poor all your lives,
miss out on the fun of America, for *this?*"
And though we know it's a false question: they'll be poor
anyway; the corporations
have paid for this broadcast, as Augustus
was "always a good-humored spectator" at the Games—

still, how we're gladdened by the countervoice
that says, so strongly it needn't be out loud,
out of the center of that flaring ring,
it has always been so; says, *if you want your life*
to mean something more than its moment, go through here.

II

Mansard Dreams

The hairy Magdalen. Your love of the emptiness. Your old lovers.
(A clacking at dawn, and the old woman calling
the pigeons, a belch of soot, to a higher mansard.)
Your dream that I'm small, in a cage, and won't eat anything
you cook me, however delicate. My dream you're a tiny dot, dancing
and your voice from somewhere else: "You can always step on it."

We wake to Paris, the long flights down, the gray.

Fine-flanged, almost heatless bedroom radiator
we had to unplug to use the one in the bathroom
without rousing the *interrompteur.*
Madame Plans, the half-Spanish concierge. The plumber-handyman,
his office his kitchen table—the door banged into it—
troisieme etage. We were on the fifth, a narrower
spidery turn below the unimaginable sixth
where the crone lived.

                    We came out one day and found her
blown into a corner like newsprint, spitting a mutter
we didn't know was addressed to us until Madame Plans,
sweeping two flights below, said *Ils sonts gentils.*
Va t'en, ferme ta gueule.
After that she'd knock at the door, when I was out,
and ask you why I did that, tap-tap-tap on the pipes,
driving her mad . . . We thought, the typewriter? But no:

I did it specially,
it seemed, between five and six in the morning.

In the shadowy side-aisle, the wooden Magdalen waited for you,
your talisman, her cascading
thicket rounding and hiding her whole body
to the knees—like ascesis, or a woman's lust
as seen by a man . . .
                            I remembered how you climbed
a tree once, beyond where I dared, and I saw your flesh
sinewed on air and the light give of branches,
suddenly free; and I thought, *she isn't like that
on land,* or should it be, *my nerves won't let her?*

Year I literally drew a box around my head
to shut out things you would say.

Year you couldn't feel we were really *here*
unless you saw it all, say, in a bus's
side-view mirror . . .

And when we broke to the streets, that Easter evening,
after working all day at being here and happy, cooking
blanquette de veau, it was like breaking prison.
I could hardly believe we'd get to the next lamp globe
in its mantilla-net of new, broad leaves
still leaning on the splendor, before it spread
too wide, in the dark waters . . .

We couldn't grasp it, somehow; now even the hot smell
of the Metro makes me happy . . .

By the end of the year, the crone knocked when *you* were out.
She'd made a discovery: *C'est votre femme qui fait ca?*
The plumber stopped answering calls. He just sat at that table
day after day. In April, he was dead.
Did he kill himself? Was it cancer? Would we have known
if my French were better, if we weren't such—*mice*!
Mansard dreams . . . Did Braque learn something from
the slight inward angle their zinc takes from the straight
wall plummeting?
Einstein says we needn't grieve, being a whole, divided
by the illusion of time. Dogen says in that dimension
you have a sixteen-foot body, solid gold.

Motel 6, Davis

Place of arrivings, goings into nowhere;
orange eye of the smoke detector overhead;
the long trucks honing in, then homing out
all night, on the long flatlands;
old couples with cookies on the dashboard,
"She'd kill me if I took a smoking room . . ."
And there is a smell, the same in all the carpets,
cool, slightly chemical, slightly tart, blue-violet
if smells had a color . . . Or if smells had words.
When my marriage was going, when no choice seemed endurable,
it made me feel loneliness was a place I could stand,
enough to take my wedding ring off and let it sit
all night on the glass shelf. And though I know
what I should say next, what everyone
knows motels are made for, I only had sex there once;
but it may honestly have been one of the best times ever,
most like the unconscious leap-dance of the movies . . .
It didn't cure the edge, though, of unlikeness
or newness between us. So I told her a story
about my daughter and me trying to iron a shirt—
not getting it right, water regurgitating—

and she said, "It makes me so happy
when you share things like that." And while it may
be true, to desire is to suffer—that long truck
or train, its halts identically hollow—
it's odd what, for different people, brings it all
to peace for a moment. Look at me—
I've wanted to write a poem about a smell,
slightly chemical, slightly tart . . . if smells had words.

Why Are We Happier?

For Paul and Jeanne Breslin

1.

Why are we happier away from home
than at home? Days take their own shape,
unwilled; because your friend's wife's sleeping in,
before you've planned the morning it's half over—
espresso bar, stripped-down brick, new styles of wintry
pale-cheeked good looks . . . The woman you met last night
might have been *right,* your age, lively not glamorous
(except she lives three thousand miles away).
At dawn your left hand finds your own firm shoulder,
untouched, in need of touching, solid-built
to run on its own tracks, like childhood trains,
however far it's meant into the future.

2.

Add on that it's the city you grew up in.
The strength of Eastern winter in the ground
comes back, as the airplane lowers, hoarding veins
of snow like silver veins in half-thawed fields.
The barbarous strength, too, of apartment brick,

with wooden outdoor porches holding on
like exposed entrails; the baseball stadium's
loneliness, from the El, the spotlight girders
high-banked on the frostbitten band of winter sunset . . .
You went to that neighborhood once, beyond your orbit,
with a coin-club friend, to a storefront where an old man
clouded old copper pennies with his fingertips
like exhaled breaths . . . The gathering dark, the unending
perspectives of those blocks
chilling you, then as now, as though your death
as well as your far birth peeked out between
forcing new channels of saying, things to say.

The Lighthouse

The Fresnel Lens works by both
refraction and reflection. Cosmic egg,
its hundreds of small crescents feed the light
down to the steady, central, eye-shaped row
that beams it twenty-four miles to the horizon.
To the Farallones where the keepers
were even more isolated; if a child was sick,
they could light a fire and hope a ship would stop,
or row their twenty-five miles to the shore.

There are facets, too, for the long-distance lovers
descending the three hundred steps and stories.
Spotting murres and seals. The silvery tinge
of the Pacific's different endlessness, Jeffers' "eye."
One says something pedantic, but the other, holding her,
feels the great beam go out to the ends of life,
shaking everything, steadying. And sometimes one of them panics
in the night, and it seems easier
to say something terribly harsh, and cut her losses.

People admire lighthouse keepers; they seem an emblem
of loneliness and steadfastness. Sometimes the sound
of the foghorn shakes the conglomerate to bits,
and they have to cement the small stones back together.

Sometimes they had to keep on
drunkards or the insubordinate; no one else
would put up with it. And once a man
was carried off the station in a straightjacket.

Linda Does My Horoscope

For Linda Wing

"Poets . . . think about fate often if not obsessively."
—Charles Baxter

"Let's not *talk* about *my* life, but the Vikings won.
It's a big deal here. In fact, I timed our call—"
"For after the game?" "*And* after the phone calls.
I've never seen a chart with so many retros."
(Retrograde planets, that from earth's perspective
seem to stop in their tracks, and then move backwards.
Ice-masses, recalcitrant, like the heavy atoms . . .)
"Retros mean . . . challenges. They *can* be opportunities.
You don't get things done the way people think they should be."

"Of course, we're not quite sure this chart is right,
if it was War Time—" Permanent Daylight Savings,
part of Prehistory, like transport planes
slowly thrumming over . . . I didn't ask my mother,
I was too embarrassed; besides, I have the feeling
I did once, and the answer was confusing.
"My hunch, knowing you, is that it *is*."

Explanations: intercepted sign, trine, ascendant . . .
The afternoon lengthens, cloudy in both cities,
both alone in our houses . . . I have—

I've had it many times—an odd
clairvoyance of my birth-hour, winter, cloudy, darkening—
not *in* the hospital, but the streets around it—
and a special hush, like . . . I'm afraid, like *Christmas* . . .

"It's an Aquarian's nature to be hopeful.
An air-sign: gets places by flying. Genius, truth-sayer,
exile. Your Sun and Moon are close—
Sun's your core essence, Moon your emotional needs—
that's good, they like each other. But, Moon in Capricorn—"

"Not great?"
        "No-o. 'Watch out, they want blood,'
this commentator says, but she's an Aries,
they don't trust earth-signs. My mother's a Moon in Capricorn,
it's not all bad. Let's see what someone else says.
'Black-dog depressions.'" "Yes." "'Deep need for love,
but guarded, paranoid. Not afraid of work.'"
Yes, yes. The years in Arlington, nothing published,
bleakness like antimatter, and wifely silence
palpable, past the study door . . .
"Capricorn moons *accomplish,* even if slowly.
It's a sea-goat, can go anywhere—swim, climb mountains . . .
They're tougher than they look, and do not lose."

"In the seventh house, all this has to do with marriage.
You like weird people—Aquarians do—
but nothing works without the intellectual connection.
Most of all you *need* a mate—though, lacking that,
a best friend will do. You'll spoil people with attention,
charming, but frightening in your dependence . . ."
B. Three weeks, no letter. N.
"Men with Moon in seven devastate women,
they're smart, and soft, and listen, listen, listen.

Placid appearance, inside hysterical—
heart on springs, reacting to how *she* reacts . . ."
Indeed, indeed.

                    "Now we come to planets.
Neptune's in Libra, but retro. Your mystical side
develops late, but will help your writing."
Sitting zazen on the stone at MacDowell, forty-three . . .
"Venus in Sagittarius, which she doesn't like,
another hint that love's going to be trouble—
freedom and commitment . . . Nothing at all
in the ninth house, and there should be. It
has to do with ultimate reputation."

So maybe this *isn't* the right chart? Or . . . a blank.

Eleventh house. Gemini. "This is the big one,
ready? You've got a *stellium* here—
three of your big planets, two of them retro,
two asteroids. Mars and Uranus
are closer still, a conjunction." (The Christmas Star?)
"Mars is your boy-planet, drive, combativeness, sparkle,
it's happy in Gemini, and likes Aquarians.
But Saturn, Uranus . . ." They come, the antimatter,
black-hole gravity, majestic, walking backwards,
that sucked years eerily
in, back, or down . . . "Shyness, inhibition."
Nontenure, nonpublication, hinterlands . . .
"Uranus—well, he's called the rude awakener."
Yes, yes. That sense of *meant to be*
that in hindsight, anyway, reconciles mortals
to almost anything.

　　　　　　　　　"Pallas near Mars
is auspicious, though—she likes war.
Here's where your Capricorn persistence comes in,
your Aquarian power to grow by leaps.
Trines, too, indicate a happy outcome."

"Trines are good, squares bad?" "Don't *say* that, I'm all squares."

More explanations. I scribble restlessly.
Two hours, my phone bill, on *astrology*!
And yet . . . I half-see them, Pallas and Mars,
swords drawn, like Walsungs, among the heavy atoms
that want blood . . .
　　　　　　　　　My mother
once said, you *smiled* so much, as a little boy.
For a moment, my two understandings—
the charmed life, the afflicted life—
come closer than they ever have, a *stellium*.

"Thank you, Linda—you've taken such *trouble*." "You're welcome.
Leos, like me, are lucky for you, but nuts.
Everything in opposition teaches."

It must be almost dark, where you are, already,
like that blessed hour . . . "Time for soup.
I hope I haven't scared you. With those planets,
you wouldn't be alive still if you hadn't
somehow learned from it, and gotten through."

Return to Boston

(Mystic River Parkway, fall 1992)

Long live the light-and-cloud of Eastern summer,
the white berries going green before they go sky-blue,
the bath of palpable air making you brother
to the moist grass, the lashing sprig . . . so that if even
a rat runs off down the bank, it only carries
another, secret part of you deeper in.

The brown water hangs its reaches, the bridge hangs its stones.

Hold onto this, day by day, running your circuit,
parkway to the traffic circle, further bridge,
farther, more urban side with the baseball field,
then the bridge home . . . Too soon it will all thin out,
dark clouds, red peaks of trees in the dark water
like broken pillars; the opposite bank
a hand's stretch away . . .

Too soon the streets close in, and things are visible
two, three blocks off, houses accordioned, serried
under the suspended snow-sky.
O now you will be tested: rust-red shingles,
white doorframes, snow shovels; samenesses people die from,
where you really live.

In Paradiso, speriamo bene

(in memory of Peter Taylor, and of Robert Lowell)

1.

Betweenspace, as I often am
in dreams, in some precise, geographical way—
one unreal street, or structure, between two real ones—
Charlottesville this time, north from the University,
suddenly you're with me, pointing out a shop window
with birds, all raptors, stuffed on dusty perches.
Their plumage mottles, dead-white to leaf-brown
to iron filings . . .

Waking, I understand: it was your generation,
the giants in the earth, who knew "the good
is the enemy of the best," and ranked the poets,
ranked their lines, even; drank till three or four,
and again at noon, and if the waiter heard them
mutter, "I really shouldn't," and turned around,
drawled majestically, "You weren't supposed to hear that . . ."

And all the more, as they grew older,
bewildered by the facade of days and buildings
no argument resolves;
each hangover breaking more blood vessels, memory-links;
the smile afloat on the body two-thirds water;

after three strokes, two decades of insulin
in public bathrooms
(delighted when a black man misunderstood, and grinned)
saying to death, "I've too many books to write . . ."

—Present moment! That sad hero,
who dies as soon as he's raised his sword and slain
all of his fathers . . . How can we live it,
knowing its guilt, and knowing
how infinitely far it's already left behind?

2.

But you showed me something else—the little vials
like Jewish Jahrzeit candles,
rosy wax sloshed and melted up their sides
over half-obliterated scripture.

You said they were poems; asked if I could say them
from memory . . .

Instead, a story: perhaps you told it to me
the first time; now, it's in his biography—

Cal was in Venice, at the Basilica
of the Frari. He wanted to see the Titian.

But his friend, angry with him
for not noticing the Madonna
a shaft of light picked out of three centuries,
because it was by *ignoto,*

told him, find it yourself.
Even he, he had to guess.

It's hard to miss: in fact, he'd described it
in a poem, long ago,
the red robes flying, "gorgeous as a jungle bird";

but he stopped a passing monk.
(One has to know, here: he botched languages
so badly, once in Paris he was given
the special seat for *mutilés de guerre*.)

Dov'è Tiziano? he asked. (Where is Titian?)

To which the monk, his finger pointing upwards:
In Paradiso, speriamo bene.

(In Paradise, we have to hope.)

Montale: Times at Bellosguardo

O how, there in the light-shot
distance that arches to the hills,
the hum of evening thins out,
and the trees begin conversing with the trite
lisp of the sandbars; how limpidly—
in a decorum
of columns and willow-alleys, among the leaping
wolves of the gardens, between the basins brimming
to overflow—this life
we hold in common, and possess no more
than breath, finds its old channel;
and how the sapphire light takes shape again
for the men
who live below there; but it is too sad
that so much peace should gather only by glints,
and everything wheel then with the rare flashes
off the misting bends; with interlacing chimneys;
with cries—fright or long laughter—off the sharp-etched
roofs, the hanging gardens; and the theater-
wings of the foliage massing; and then the whole
luminous coda trailed to heaven, before
desire could find the words!

*

Desolate, exposed
on the low hill
magnolia foliage: brownish-
green if the wind carries
with the ground-floor chill a distorted
rushing of harmonies,
and every leaf that vibrates
and kindles in the thicket,
drinks to its last fibre
the greeting; and more desolate
the foliage of the living
who lose their way
in the prism of the minute,
the limbs vowed to a brief
circle of fever, a motion
always the same: sweat that comes
with the pulse, and the death-sweat; acts
minutes mirrored, refracting
echoes of the battering that above
facets the sun to the rain;
pendulum swing between life
that goes each second and life
always the same; and even
up here, no release: you die
knowingly or choose life
that changes and is ignorant: another death.
And the cradle goes down between the loggias
and the busts on pillars: the harmony awakens
the stones that have seen the great
images, honor,
inflexible love, the wager,
faith that does not bend.

And the gesture remains: to measure
the emptiness, sound its boundaries;
the unknown gesture that expresses
oneself and no one else: the ever-living
passion one blood, one brain
that cannot be repeated; and perhaps it enters
what closes us and forces it with a slender
picklock's point.

*

The broken-rooftile crackle of the storm
in the dilated air not yet split open,
the list of the tricuspid
Canada poplar in the garden, shaken
at every gust—
and the sign? of a life that underpins
the marble at each stepping-stone as the ivy
distrusts the solitary
push of the bridges I uncover, climbing;
of an hourglass not of sand but works, measures,
faces and footfalls of men;
of water combed out under the pavilions
and no longer quick-tempered to try soundings
of volcanic stone . . . all vanished? And the rooftiles
give their long sound; the palings barely
defend the ellipse of the convolvuli,
grasshoppers rain from the pergola on our books,
shake themselves, and limp off. And so a hard
labor, celestial weavers, is cut off
on the frame of men. As for tomorrow . . .

Montale: Ti libero la fronte

I free your forehead of the icicles
you gathered crossing the high nebulae,
and the feathers lacerated in the long
cyclones. You wake with a frightened start.

Midday: the medlar lengthens its black
shadow on the panelling; a shivery sun
persists in the sky. And the other shadows, those turning
the corner in the alley, have no idea you're here.

Puccini Dying

I could not find the music
that would marry
the hero to the ice-princess in this life.

Her music came easy: mirror-shock, avalanche
of desire and pride retreating
to the inner cave: sleep that perfumes the world . . .
And the other's, the slave girl's,
who stands for
flesh and devotion, and must be sacrificed.

And *his* voice, that believes it could persuade anything.

. . . It was perhaps the one time I really *wasn't* guilty.
We really were just having a cigarette together
at the foot of the stairs
after late cleaning-up, and late scribbling.
But my wife threw her out; went and talked to the priest;
screamed *whore* when they met in the public street.

Her family sued; barricaded themselves in their house;
I fled to Paris. Then Doria
swallowed a corrosive
and took five days to die.
The doctors examined the body, and pronounced her *virgo intacta.*

I said I would never live with Elvira again
after that. But I did. Perhaps
I needed to look in the earth's stony mirror
to know myself . . . Perhaps
I was too much at home with executioners.

The Prince of Persia goes by, and the moon rises;
his head is shown. Liu goes off, draped over
a little Tartar horse, like an old figurine,
and the old king follows . . .

Next month
they will take me to Brussels, make a hole in my throat,
and stick seven radium needles in the cancer.

My secret was simple: to circle a note, above, then below,
stands for longing,
the way people will sit and watch wave after wave at the shore.

Now there is a man who says
you must not repeat a note
until every note in the whole scale has been sounded.
They are driving me to Firenze, in my new Lancia,
to hear him. Perhaps he
and the blind old king will lead me
into the toneless *night that has no morning.*

The Canto of Hope
(Paradiso XXV, 1–9)

For Robert Pinsky

Should it ever happen, that this sacred verse,
to which both heaven and earth have set their hands,
so that it kept me lean for many years,

prove stronger than the cruelty that bans
me from the lovely sheepfold where I dreamt
myself its warlords' enemy—the lamb

an enemy to the wolf!—with what a different
voice, and different fleece, I shall return
a poet, and beside the very font

where I was baptized, take the laurel crown.

Ikkyu

(after Sonja Arntzen)

1) In the moment of his enlightenment, he thinks of his mother, driven from the imperial court.

For ten years, hurled this way and that by anger—
now a crow laughs, I leave the dust behind.
Though the sun still shines on the palace of no returning,
the jade-like face sings.

2) On interdependence:

Why do they call the little rock the bride of the island?
The woman who came to the Emperor in a dream
said, "In the morning I am cloud, in the evening rain."
If I am not at T'ien-t'ai, I shall be at Nan-yueh.
The bare post exhausts the day, coming and going.

3) The Fish-Basket Kuanon.

Kuanon, in one story, became a fisherman's wife,
wondering at her feelings in the dream of cloud-rain.
Her thousand eyes of Compassion were looked at but not seen.
And yet—a wife by the water,
red cheeks, blue-black hair; a whole life of song!

4) His "elder brother" gives their teacher many posthumous honors.

Daito begged under a bridge for twenty years.
Fragrant titles, eternal fame—what kind of Zen is that?
There was a king in China, once, who behaved very badly,
he had his enemy's corpse dug up and flogged three hundred times.

5) He resigns his sub-abbotship and leaves Daitoku-ji, pinning this note to his door: "Look for me in the taverns and the fish-shops, / if you don't find me there, try a brothel."

Those who keep the rules are donkeys, those who break the rules are men.
Before conception, the child falls in love with his parents from heaven.
When chaos was not yet separated, the darkness was pitch-black,
the clouds and moon knew for whom they were beautiful.

6) He lives in retirement in the mountains.

When I spread horse-dung, I feel at one with Lan-t'san
who did not seek fame and fortune. Wind flowing away.
Mutual longing without end. Wives waiting beside a river,
their tears gave the mottled bamboo its spots.
Wang Hui-chih planted bamboo before he furnished his house,
saying, "How can I live a day without this lord?"

7) To Mori, a blind singer, the love of his old age:

Blind Mori plays when I want to sing in the evenings.
Under the covers, we talk all night, never bored.
Mandarin ducks sleep out their remaining life on the water.
We have promised to meet again in the time of Maitreya.
But this old Buddha has seen ten thousand springs.

8) In his old age, Daitoku-ji burned to the ground in the Onin War, he is
persuaded to become abbot.

Daito's descendants exhausted his remaining light.
Hard to melt the heart in song, this icy night, in the ruins.
For fifty years, I begged in my straw raincoat.
I feel ashamed putting on this purple robe.

Almost at the Horizon

For M.

Something in the world
is turning from me. The strange beepers,
like a flock of small birds, that make crossing-lights
safe for the blind. This young man reading us
his story about the goodbye in the morning square,
where nothing can be said because what could be has happened
in a movie already, so he watches their clothes instead
and the other people watching. Something in all this
must feel sexy to him, his short black hair is so carefully
slicked aside, with a little wave. The air
is fresh and cool in the morning, the new buildings
cubic and lucent. Like Hopper, but feelingless.
But perhaps the feeling is just invisible, the way a ship
slipping over the horizon has no hull any more
only masts. Is that how one knows
where one stands on the earth is
slipping east, not to be slowed now? Except
almost at the horizon
your clear eyes.

The Wall of June

Summer hovers over us, like the rock-wall
over the cliff dwelling on this month's calendar,
a heat too heavy to move with, a larger skull
over the little house of eyes and mouth,
not thinking . . .
          The days
slip by too indistinguishable, never enough
time spent working the earth; the garden chairs
we never sat in enough far too hot now,
the weeds full grown.

            The plan to read
a French poem every evening . . .

Not a season, but the apex of seasons . . .
We have to remind ourselves where we are in it, like a boat
out of sight of both continents.
               Even its end
won't come visibly at first, a golden thickening
at the edge of the light, like gold on a leaf
or shoreward algae . . .

         On the daybed
a few scattered pages, a longer print-out
remain.

Caitlin: A Biography

The wild white hair in your ears making you look
like a baleful owl; the frail, belligerent eyes
like some gray poet—Baudelaire, in the etching—
affronted by Time, Old Age, Death and the World.
Your low-slung, widening waddle, from behind
is like what animal? Skunk? Raccoon? A *badger*!
—A badger's, too, your sudden bite.

Later, your head comes knocking against my elbow;
half-averted, your sorrowful, affectionate gaze . . .

We're none of us responsible
for our childhoods. Wild kitten from Lake Temescal,
found starving by the rangers who had your mother spayed . . .
Your thirteenth year, I sit beside you and say, "I knew you
when you were a bundle of fleas. Anne wanted
to send you back to be fumigated." (*Snarl.*)
"But 'all beings by nature are Buddha.' " (And, slowly, *purr.*)

Of course, Anne *felt* the bites; E. and I didn't—
easy for us to moralize! So you lived
six months alone in the "activity room,"
the storeroom, really . . . Let loose in the morning,
you'd lie in ambush for the smallest of us
to venture down the stairs.

The divorce meant
five houses for you, too. And then the one
that made you an indoor cat again brought also
the Interloper, that ridiculous miniature,
yellow, endlessly friendly, endlessly curious eyes.
Clear enough, to you: she hadn't a *soul;* you did.

(Whatever one is. What Christian ever measured
his hopes for a second life
by the similitude of your eyes, ears, nose and brain?
Hindus gave you a second chance. Buddhists, "All beings"
etc. notwithstanding, shrewder: you
the only animal that refused to come,
when Shakyamuni was dying, to say goodbye.)

Perhaps a soul is this: a small refraction
of the great shadows moving us from above,
a knowing more than one knows—one block of Berkeley,
interrupted by rooms in Evanston, in Vermont . . .
This much I'll say: you are
a person; you can purr and growl at once.
Mnnrao, you complain
("Crying *What I do is me: for that I came*")
out of your daylong slumber on my bed.

Dinosaurs

(after the PBS series)

At the far end of an upstairs wing, and scarier
for the way the long hall darkened toward its midpoint,
just where the ribcage rounded overhead
and the neckbones began their climb. Of course he couldn't
come alive; but if he did? On the high walls
strange waters, limber palms, filled out his world,
and the huge haunches, gray and thick as *Sinclair*
motor oil, crunched them down. Surfacing through time,
more bones, and dioramas. By the exit
a sabertooth has trapped itself
chasing a glytodont into a tar-pit.

And Como Bluff, "Graveyard of the Dinosaurs"—
Highway 30 still two-lane—whose gloomy profile,
more than the sign, made me drag my parents into
a wind-silvered, raw-board shack, to buy ribbed bits of
something wilder, even, than being there, on that road.
I missed it, this year, on I-80; now the TV
confirms it, and the two scientists who fought over it,
the one who died first bequeathing his skull
to a museum, just to prove his brain was bigger.

We thought *their* brains were too small; that's why they died—
and depending too much on the extra one, in the tail.
Now it's not so clear. Between their age
and the start of ours, there's a thin layer of marl—
the same in a dozen countries—with *glass*
in it, and outer-space minerals, and metal droplets
thinning like the crest-ring from a splash in milk;
which made them start looking for the great rock that's shown here
wheeling in from space, rough and so brilliant
it dissolves to a ray of dots, a computer-map.
Then the globe shawls itself in fire.

Strange, in ten years to have learned a way of doom
we never thought of, when we thought of everything—
plague, nuclear winter, the Son come in His Glory.
And always out there . . . One dazzled over western
Colorado, a few years back, then swung up, missing
earth and the headlines.
                              And hardly less
strange, the millions of years that didn't need us,
our kind of mind. The huge herds of
Triceratops, like bison, roaming the endless plains,
that wouldn't, of course, be *Triceratops*
for sixty million more years. Shall we say, they had Buddha-nature?
Did the rock, whirling from space, have Buddha-nature?

Why do we smile, then, to know such things existed,
ran gracefully, even, over the face of the planet,
its new face we'll never see? With the first flowers
upon it, to scatter their quick alphabet
before the slow teeth, used to palms.

If the rock wheels on us from beyond the night,
what I'd wish for is that something, somewhere,
half-guess your lineaments and find them lovable,
as I find the animator's duckbills, lifting
their placid heads to watch the big thing lowering
bright, then darker, behind the bands of cloud.

After "Death of a Porn Queen": Traveling the Great Basin

Everyone wants to sleep with a girl from a small town.
No one wants to be a girl from a small town,
facing the choices—waitress, wife, switchboard girl.
A difficulty of Being, and its elsewheres.
So the beautiful ones—boys, too—move on, and play themselves
in huge light, if they're lucky; if not, a hotel bedroom.
And those left behind carry the heaviness
of the body, the dingy hallway
where no one cleans the paint-drips off the Western mural.

Towns with their white initials on the hills,
towns that still seem an echo of the mountains,
plangent, purple at sunset, rock of another planet
over the far-off cat's-eye of the trains . . .
But no one wants to end in the graveyard at Winnemucca,
unfenced, no hedge even, gravel, a few low trees,
the statues' glare like junked cars'—a part of the lift to the ranges . . .

Red Cloud

                              The cat
had to come into restaurants. She was too rare,
there were "catnappers." So your parka went down over
the carrying-case, like a parrot's silence-cloth,
and you gripped the handle through it, hoped the waitress
kept her eyes up, on me.
                        It worked, oddly—she knew
when not to mew—except one off-hour dinner . . .

In between, sharp Abyssinian ears
back and forth in the rearview mirror.

                                        *

Power plant past Reno, with four white blinkers
on the tallest stack to warn low-flying planes;
and then the hills fold down . . . always the gateway
to the earlier country where slow freights stretch out
a mile or two in the Sinks; where gypsum chutes
rise through openwork toward rust-iron roofs . . .
Rock Springs where you wrote down a conversation
between two bullet-heads, in the Chinese
railroad-car diner, and the cat kept quiet:
"horseflies in Texas—stung the cattle to death—
but you could drown them in oildrums filled with beer—"
"AIDS—should stay in Africa—they started it . . ."

You said, too, one night, "We never talk, just argue"—
my travel nerves, bad as my father's—

*

To Cather, transplanted from Virginia,
an erasure of personality . . . the roads
petering out in bunch grass, land *bare as a piece of sheet iron.*
When a lark flew up, she couldn't stop herself crying.
All her life she feared going back, even drowsing off
in a cornfield, in case she happened to die there.
But when *the country and I had it out,* she was *gripped*
with a passion I have never shaken.

The writer
fades away into the land and people of his heart.
He dies of love only to be born again.

*

We're here. Bald brick of the one-crossroads town—
our one pause, in your five-day rush home to school—
with little Romanesque or Arab zigzags
out of the brick itself, or out of red stone,
or white capstones on the windows—Dr. Archie's
second-story office, we've found it, there's a plaque—
and the turreted, townhouse-size bank, the "Cather Museum" . . .
You compose your pictures, your first way of focusing
on anything at all, this summer . . .

The streets themselves cobbled with brick. In the background, always,
the flat hot sky . . . as if it were a law that the soul
has to feed on what is most unlike it; that creation
begins in erasure—not just this place, but all Being
slipping past the horizon a block away.

*

Upstairs was *ours,* the children said. No grown-up
ever came up there—the unplaned beams and rafters,
the siblings' cots, and then the nook she finally
made wholly her own, with the red-and-brown-rose wallpaper . . .
She dragged her bed to the window, hot summer nights
she'd rather have been out walking—*as if her heart were spreading
all over the desert . . . vibrating with
excitement, as a machine vibrates with speed.*

You especially want to photograph that dimness,
but it's too strong in the end—the roses indistinguishable
from old tears in the paper . . .

*In reality, life rushes
from within, not without. There is no work so beautiful
it was not once all contained in some youthful body, trembling.*

*

The soul has to learn about cruelty.
                        Vivisection,
her "favorite amusement"; her high school speech in praise of it
still framed, in the bank, past the old-fashioned teller's
brass bars . . .

                    The old doctor
took the girl on his rounds in the buggy, let her give
the chloroform once.

After that . . . to be inside
another being's skin, actually *see* the blood flow past . . .

Was it shadow-revenge, outrush of power
in one who'd lost so much? (Biographers tell us
a boy once threatened to cut off her hand.)

Or an indecency native to art?

—A taste, at any rate, she eventually
gave the worst man she ever wrote about,
then gave him her loveliest woman.

                              *

Towards sundown. The trackless "Cather Prairie"
just before the sign on the empty road says "Kansas";
but we don't get far in its messy, spiky tangles . . .
Why still so vivid?

                    I was losing the power
to read your face, its doughiness, its charm
more opaque, this puberty summer—fearing each bad moment,
each dinner I was silent through, or snappish,
might become permanent . . .

                    And already enough
sense of destiny a kind of iron clenches
in your voice when you say, "It's so hard to be good at anything,
good so it matters . . ."

But still, this twilight,
by the locked Depot—you wandering, taking pictures
from the weeds, the disused spurs—there's such peace in the air
I might be your age again, or She
still holding it all—the stationmaster's chair
sealed up, fifty years?—in her vast, impersonal eye . . .

Three bows, down to the dirt, palms lifted over
my head
            I won't make here, but two months later,
by her grave in the icicle warps of crisp New England
fall morning light . . .

The world is bare as a piece of sheet iron. And no work
was not once contained in some youthful body, trembling.

Notes

"The Cusp, " p. 4
"Todd Gitlin": cf. *The Sixties: Years of Hope, Days of Rage* (New York: Bantam Books, 1987), pp. 1–2.

"Dreams of Sacrifice," p. 6
Cf. Alan Williamson, "Two Faces," *Poetry Northwest,* Autumn 1972.

"Listening to Leonard Cohen," p. 11
"In the dawn of time": cf. Wordsworth, *The Prelude,* Book XI, ll. 108–9.
    I did live through the end of the 1960s in Charlottesville, Virginia. Beulah and Ulro are Blakean terms: Beulah, roughly, the Earthly Paradise we discover when the imagination invests itself in the external world and the external world reveals hidden depths; Ulro the Hell we fall into when we live by unexamined imaginative premises, believing we live only by materialistic pragmatism. Blake was much in the minds of many people, particularly many academics, drawn to the counterculture, as a precedent for our way of thinking within the received canon.
"There is a grain of sand": Blake, *Jerusalem,* Plate 37, ll. 15–19, Plate 35, ll. 1–2.
"heroes in the seaweed," etc.: cf. Leonard Cohen, "Suzanne."
"Oh Lord": Janis Joplin, "Mercedes Benz."
"I saw a beggar": Leonard Cohen, "Bird on a Wire."
The "Jesus freaks," as we called them, did actually picket a lecture by R. D. Laing in Charlottesville, with the leaflet described.

"Altamont," p. 14
Cf. Todd Gitlin, *The Sixties,* pp. 406–7, and Richard Tillinghast, "The Grateful Dead: Questions of Survival," *Michigan Quarterly Review* 30, no. 4: 686–98.

Peter: Peter Dale Scott.

"Speakers from the Ice, " p. 17
Cf. *Inferno,* XXXIII–XXXIV. The poem also owes a debt to Molly Giles's great story, "Talking to Strangers."

"Limit of Volume," p. 21
"Antichrist in the kitchen": Tori Amos, "Silent All These Years." *"In Utero"*: Cobain's last album.

"*La Pastorela*," p. 23
Hispanic Christmas play, performed every other year at the Mission in San Juan Bautista by the Teatro Campesino, a group which had its origins in Cesar Chavez's United Farm Workers movement. A few years ago there was a televised version, with an elaborate frame-story (retold, in part, in the poem), and with Linda Ronstadt as the Archangel Michael. The stories referred to in l. 6, and in the next-to-last stanza, were much in the news in 1992 and 1993.

"Mansard Dreams," p. 31
"Einstein": cf. Jon Kabat-Zinn, *Full Catastrophe Living* (New York: Delta, 1990), p. 165. "Dogen": "The Time-Being," *Moon in a Dewdrop* (Berkeley, CA: North Point Press, 1985).

"*In Paradiso, speriamo bene,*" p. 45
"It's in his biography": cf. Paul Mariani, *Lost Puritan* (New York: W. W. Norton, 1994), pp. 379–80. "Gorgeous as a jungle bird": Lowell, "Beyond the Alps."

"Puccini Dying," p. 52
Puccini did stop writing *Turandot* more or less at the point where Timur follows Liu's corpse offstage; the concluding love duet was completed, from his notes, by Alfano. The Doria story, and the story of his late trip to Firenze to hear Schoenberg, can be found in Mosco Carner's *Puccini* (New York: Knopf, 1959).

"Ikkyu," p. 55
Ikkyu is my favorite of the Zen poets because he is the most outrageous; also because he has a wistful, nostalgic streak than runs counter to our calm, "mellow" image of Zen. He is supposed to have been the illegitimate son of the Emperor. He hated rules and ceremonies, drank, and had many love affairs. To this day the abbot of his monastery within Daitoku-ji is allowed to wear plain black robes, rather than ceremonial ones, in his memory.

In making this biographical collage, I have borrowed, with permission, from Sonja Arntzen's definitive translations and even more from her prose commentary. Sometimes I have merged two poems into one, or unfolded an allusion that would have been tacitly clear to the original audience.

"Caitlin: A Biography," p. 60
"Crying *What I do*": Gerard Manley Hopkins, "As Kingfishers Catch Fire."

"Red Cloud," p. 66
All quotes come either from Willa Cather, *The Song of the Lark,* or from James Woodress's *Willa Cather: A Literary Life* (Lincoln: University of Nebraska Press, 1987), or Sharon O'Brien's *Willa Cather: The Emerging Voice* (New York: Oxford University Press, 1987).

Three bows: a Zen observance, lifting the feet of Buddha over one's head.